This Amazing Wally Annual belongs to:

....

Published by Ladybird Books Ltd 2012
A Penguin Company
Penguin Books Ltd, 80 Strand, London, WC2R 0RL, UK
Penguin Books Australia Ltd, Camberwell, Victoria, Australia
Penguin Group (NZ), 67 Apollo Drive, Auckland, 0632, New Zealand
(a division of Pearson New Zealand Ltd)

Sunbird is a trade mark of Ladybird Books Ltd

Written by Mandy Archer
'A Diamond in the Rough' drawn by Duncan Smith
Neil Armstrong (page19) and map of the moon (page 47)
courtesy of NASA

002 – 10 9 8 7 6 5 4 3 2

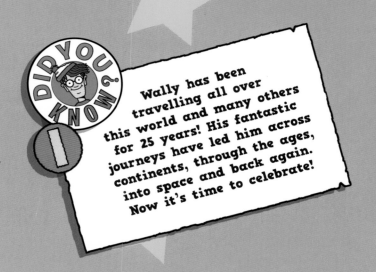

DID YOU KNOW?

Wally has been travelling all over this world and many others for 25 years! His fantastic journeys have led him across continents, through the ages, into space and back again. Now it's time to celebrate!

CONTENTS

Hey, Wally fans!

Welcome to my official annual — packed from the first page to the last with fun, facts and games to amuse Wally Watchers and their pals! This special silver-jubilee edition will delight and divert armchair explorers the world over.

So let's go!

Romp through puzzles, stories, make-its and mind-boggling amazing facts, then get ready for an epic game of search-and-find. There are 25 special party guests to locate, plus a head-spinning bounty of hidden kit to hunt for listed on pages 8, 20 and 61.

No Wally annual would be complete without a jam-tastic scene to pore over! Join the party in the centre pages, then take a look for me, Woof, Wenda, Wizard Whitebeard and Odlaw*. Woof's as shy as ever — only his tail gives him away!

25 years on the road deserves an epic celebration. Come along and enjoy the ride!

Wally

*Don't forget about my lost key, Woof's bone, Wenda's camera, Wizard Whitebeard's scroll and Odlaw's binoculars too!

DID YOU KNOW?

2

The first person to circumnavigate the globe without using electrical or engine power was Mike Horn in 2000. The South African took 513 days to make the round trip on foot, bicycle, canoe and sailing trimaran.

WHO'S WHO?

ALL YOUR OLDEST PALS ARE WAITING TO MEET AND GREET YOU! THE EXCITEMENT BEGINS RIGHT HERE . . .

WALLY

Wally is a world traveller, always in search of the next adventure! Whether at the beach, in Hollywood or in the Stone Age, Wally loves to observe his surroundings and has a passion for trivia and uncovering facts. You'll recognise this globetrotter by his iconic wardrobe. Wally always travels light, but never on his own.

WOOF

Woof is Wally's best friend and his most loyal companion. He can sniff out danger in a flash and he's hot on the trail for his lost bone. Have you seen it? Wherever Wally goes, Woof is never far behind, but you can only see his tail, unless you're in "The Land of Woofs".

WENDA

Wenda is one of Wally's closest friends who shares his uncanny knack for fashionable attire. She is a fellow explorer and a keen photographer, always recording the action and fun on their journeys . . . when her camera isn't misplaced, that is.

WIZARD WHITEBEARD

Wizard Whitebeard is Wally's magical mentor. With limitless wisdom and common sense, he sends Wally off on his incredible journeys. Despite the Wizard's vast powers, it seems he has lost track of his enchanted scroll . . . again.

ODLAW

Odlaw is Wally's sneaky alter ego. Devious to the core, he is obsessed with thwarting Wally at every turn. But luckily it's Odlaw's plans that usually wind up getting foiled. If you find his missing binoculars, be sure to pick them up. After all, it's better to spot Odlaw before he spots you!

THE WALLY WATCHERS

Wherever Wally goes, a host of Wally Watchers are sure to be seen trailing behind. A true Watcher wears red and white on top, teamed with blue bottoms and walking boots. This loyal crew always try their best to keep up, desperate to savour every adventure from start to finish.

The hunt is on! Earn your stripes by finding the following 100 thing within these pages.

At Wally's Celebration

1. Wally
2. Wenda
3. Woof's tail
4. Wizard Whitebeard
5. Odlaw
6. 25 uniformed band members
7. Little Bo Peep
8. A man with a present for a head
9. 25 pink envelopes
10. A ladle
11. A boxer
12. A music-loving robin
13. A toy yacht
14. A fisherman with a big catch
15. A miner's lamp
16. 25 Wally Watchers
17. John's director's chair
18. A Wally scarf
19. A large cupcake
20. A man reading a book about gorillas
21. A saxophone blowing bubbles
22. A purple, blue and green piece of cake
23. 3 people with birds in their hair

24. 25 party guests in animal costumes
25. A bell
26. A Roman soldier
27. 5 basketball players
28. Acrobats helping themselves to cake
29. A clown with a cherry nose
30. A man wearing 3 party hats
31. A gondolier with no gondola
32. A scroll
33. A lady waving her handkerchief
34. Little Red Riding Hood
35. The 25 party guests from the front of the book
36. Sherlock Holmes and Dr Watson
37. A man balancing 4 slices of cake
38. A TV presenter with a picture of Wally
39. A little girl with a red lolly
40. 25 green cherries
41. A pencil and ruler in a pocket
42. 6 forks
43. A cheerleader with pom-poms
44. 25 number 25s
45. A paint palette
46. A heart-shaped balloon
47. Some tadpoles

48. 2 royals fencing

49. A slithering snake

50. A man with a present shaped like a bird

51. 2 ladies with their hair tied in red spotty scarves

52. 2 men with their fingers in their ears

53. A spanner

54. 3 men sharing a moustache

55. Woof's bone

56. A piece of cake with a flower on it

57. A man with a big pink present

58. A slice of cake on a unicorn's horn

59. A spear with a piece of cake on the end

60. A sword

61. A crazy drinking straw

62. An artist mouse

63. 3 pitchforks

64. A daisy hat

65. A large key

66. A small key

67. A goldfish bowl

68. 4 plant pots

69. A fighter pilot

70. A telescope

71. A man wearing headphones

72. An American footballer

73. A piece of cake with a heart on it

74. A queen

75. An alarm clock

Elsewhere in the Annual

76. 5 astronomical balloons in Whitebeard's bunch

77. 2 zeppelins

78. A ballerina blending in with the Wally Watchers

79. A red boat with a yellow sail

80. A spanner-shaped balloon

81. A hat holding up 2 noses

82. 2 painters

83. 5 transport balloons in Whitebeard's bunch

84. Wally with Odlaw's legs

85. A Viking-helmet balloon

86. A lock and key from Wally's bag

87. A blue bow tie with white polka dots

88. 5 balloon bones in Whitebeard's bunch

89. A snowman in a witch's hat

90. A cowboy with stars on his hat

91. Balloons numbered 1 to 9 in Whitebeard's bunch

92. A witch in a cowboy hat

93. A pirate-cutlass balloon

94. A red flower with 7 petals

95. 5 pink invitations clutched by a crowd

96. An island with 2 palm trees

97. Odlaw peeking round a page

98. A guitar-shaped balloon

99. A Watcher with 2 aliens

100. A witch's-hat balloon

DID YOU KNOW?

3

If you transported the entire population of Manhattan in New York to Alaska, each person would have twelve acres to themself.

PUZZLED PACKING

Wally's old-fashioned rucksack is small on the outside, but it's an even tighter squeeze on the inside. Over the years, he's perfected the art of travelling light. When you're on the road, every piece of kit has got to count! Unscramble the anagrams to decipher what objects come out top of Wally's packing list each and every time.

1. PNOSEG to keep things wet.
Sponge

2. GMINYFINAG SASGL to help you take a closer look.
Magnifying glass

3. CHROT to shed light on new situations.
Torch

4. LEPCIN for when a picture says a thousand words.
Pencil

5. ERIC to keep things dry.
Rice

6. DOPRSSACT so you never lose touch.
Postcards

7. ATEP to mend and make do.
Tape

8. NACHAROMI to keep a song in your heart.
Harmonica

9. YENNP to make sure you'll never be broke.
Penny

10. RAE SPLUG for a dreamy night's sleep.
Ear plugs

DID YOU KNOW?

4

The Mazda Suitcase Car did exactly what it said on the tin! In 1991, engineers at Mazda designed a three-wheel car that folded down into a standard size suitcase. The car had a 40cc engine that could reach speeds of 43 km/h, holding enough fuel for two hours' of driving time.

DOWN MEMORY LANE

Do you have an eye for detail? Wally's old leather satchel has spilled across this page. Study the spread of souvenirs, snacks and survival gear for two minutes, then turn the page to pit your wits against the best Wally Watchers in the land. Can you crack all 25 questions and become the eagle-eyed, super-spotting champ?

PTO

DOWN MEMORY LANE

Can you outsmart the Wally Watchers when it comes to extreme observation?
Find a pen and paper, take a deep breath, and then start!

1. Who features on the postage stamp?
2. How many items of food were in the picture?
3. What colour is the button?
4. Is the soldier facing left or right?
5. How many forms of transport are there?
6. What colour is the icing on the cake?
7. Does the paintbrush have paint on it?
8. Is the padlock locked or unlocked?
9. How many red stripes does the candy cane have?
10. Which other item has red stripes?
11. Is the envelope open or closed?
12. What colour is the envelope?
13. Which way is the compass pointing?
14. Which item commonly used by doctors is there?
15. What colour is the thread in the needle?
16. The rocket is red, blue and which other colour?
17. What number is on the top of the die?
18. What other two numbers are also visible on the die?
19. What colour is the soldier's jacket?
20. How many petals does the flower have?
21. Which three letters are on the block?
22. How many stitches are on the ball?
23. What two colours are the stripes on the tie?
24. How many points does the wand star have?
25. Who is peeking around the corner of the page?

Truly foxed, flummoxed and flabbergasted? Strugglers can turn back for one 30-second refresh. After that, no peeking is permitted!

TREKKING TIPS

Planes, trains and fast cars are all very well, but nothing beats the pleasure of roaming on foot! Wally's rambles give him the freedom to take detours, discover new places and experience the best (and worst) that nature has to offer. Don't rush from place-to-place with your nose glued to a guidebook; slow down and savour the world around you!

Making tracks

Even city travellers are never far away from some eye-popping wildlife! Rediscover the ancient art of tracking, looking out for the clues that animals leave behind. In days gone by, our European ancestors used this vital skill to find food and stay safe from attack, but the method is still used in many parts of the world.

Step outside your door with a magnifying glass and a torch. What can you see? Discarded nut shells and husks? Animal droppings? Prints in the snow, mud or sand, and scratch marks on trees?

Now the analysis really starts! Does the track have claws? Is it bumpy, arched or smooth? Measure and record your discovery in a notebook, take a photo, or make a cast in plaster of Paris.

Follow the stars

Nowadays we can flick on sat navs and pick up GPS signals on our phones, but it hasn't always been this way. Since ancient times, travellers have used the stars to find their way. If you can find North, you've got all the information that you need to work out the points in the compass. In the Northern Hemisphere, it all starts with Polaris - the North Star.

The simplest way to track down Polaris is to find its brighter, neighbouring constellation, the Big Dipper. The Big Dipper is a formation of seven stars that look like a giant ladle in the sky. Now trace an imaginary line up from the last two points in the scoop of the ladle and you'll see a fainter star glowing above it. This is Polaris.

While the other stars are slowly turning above our heads, Polaris is fixed, making it the ideal navigation point.

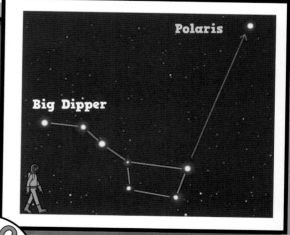

Brilliant bushcraft

How do the Wally Watchers keep up with the great traveller's circuitous routes, crazy cutbacks and daft detours? Some say that Wally leaves signposts to help his pals find their way. Next time you go exploring with friends, split into two groups. Set the first group off fifteen minutes' early, asking them to leave a trail for the second group to follow. Can you both make it along the same route, using natural markers to show the way?

DID YOU KNOW?

5 Laos is the only land-locked country in Asia. Trekking can be treacherous here; Laos is covered with dense forest and dizzyingly high mountain peaks!

HOW TO DRAW WALLY

With just a few circles and some wobbly lines you can draw a wonderful Wally! Follow the steps here in pencil or pen using bold, thick lines.

①

②

③

④

⑤

⑥

⑦

Add colour and, hey presto, here I am! Why not invent a head of your own?

15

BALLOON GAME!

Wizard Whitebeard has conjured up a brilliant batch of balloons for Wally's party! His beard meanders through the bunch, but which balloon is it tied to?

THE TRAVELLERS' HALL OF FAME

They came, they saw, they conquered! Wally is the latest in a noble line of fearless explorers who opened our eyes to the wonders of the world.

The curiosity of man has taken us up mountain peaks, over turbulent oceans and through the most extreme conditions that weather can wield. Here are some of Wally's favourite intrepid travellers, but there are plenty more out there. Who inspires you to get out and see the world firsthand?

Jason and the Argonauts

Born: Asia Minor
Lived: around 1500 BCE

Claim to fame:
Historical records and ancient myths suggest that Jason chartered a ship in search of golden fleeces. He had the courage to voyage out of the known world, across the Dead Sea.

Fascinating fact:
When a sheep's fleece is stretched across a wooden frame and flushed with water, tiny shards of gold cling to the wool. This inspired legends that have lasted for generations.

Leif Erikson

Born: Iceland
Lived: 970 CE-1020 CE

Claim to fame:
After setting up colonies in Greenland, Viking explorer Leif embarked on an epic voyage. He is widely regarded as the first European to land in North America, 500 years before Christopher Columbus.

Fascinating fact:
Leif was the Viking son of Erik the Red.

Marco Polo

Born: Italy
Lived: 1254-1324

Claim to fame:
Marco Polo landed his place in the history books when he ventured east along the Silk Road, all the way to the court of Kublai Khan, the Mongol Ruler of China.

Fascinating fact:
During the 18th and 19th centuries, many historians found it hard to believe the sensational sights and experiences that Polo wrote about.

James Cook

Born: England
Lived: 1728-1799

Claim to fame:
Captain James Cook rose up through the ranks of the navy to lead three epic sea voyages across the vast Pacific Ocean.

Fascinating fact:
Cook landed in Botany Bay on the east coast of Australia in 1770. He claimed the strange land for Britain, naming it New South Wales. The Captain later discovered the islands of Hawaii too.

Jacques-Yves Cousteau

Born: France
Lived: 1910-1997

Claim to fame:
Jacques Cousteau devoted his life to exploring the sea. He converted an old mine-sweeper ship called the *Calypso* into an ocean laboratory, spending years writing and broadcasting about his discoveries.

Fascinating fact:
Cousteau so loved being in the water, he was sometimes nicknamed the 'manfish'. In 1943, Cousteau also assisted in inventing the Aqua Lung.

Neil Armstrong

Born: USA
Lived: 1930-present day

Claim to fame:
Neil Armstrong helped his country win the space race, when the astronaut took his first momentous step on the Moon. *Apollo 11* landed on the lunar surface on 20 July 1969.

Fascinating fact:
Armstrong's first moonwalk was watched by over a billion people!

The spectators at this gallery have swapped some items of clothing! Can you work out who has swapped with who?

DID YOU KNOW?

7

We might think that we've got the world charted, mapped and plotted, but there's still so much more for mankind to discover! Only recently one of the world's largest lakes was found beneath the ice sheets of Antarctica. Scientists are using probes to drill down into Lake Vostok's 15-million-year-old waters.

FANTASTIC 50

Continue the search with 50 more fun things to find at Wally's celebration!

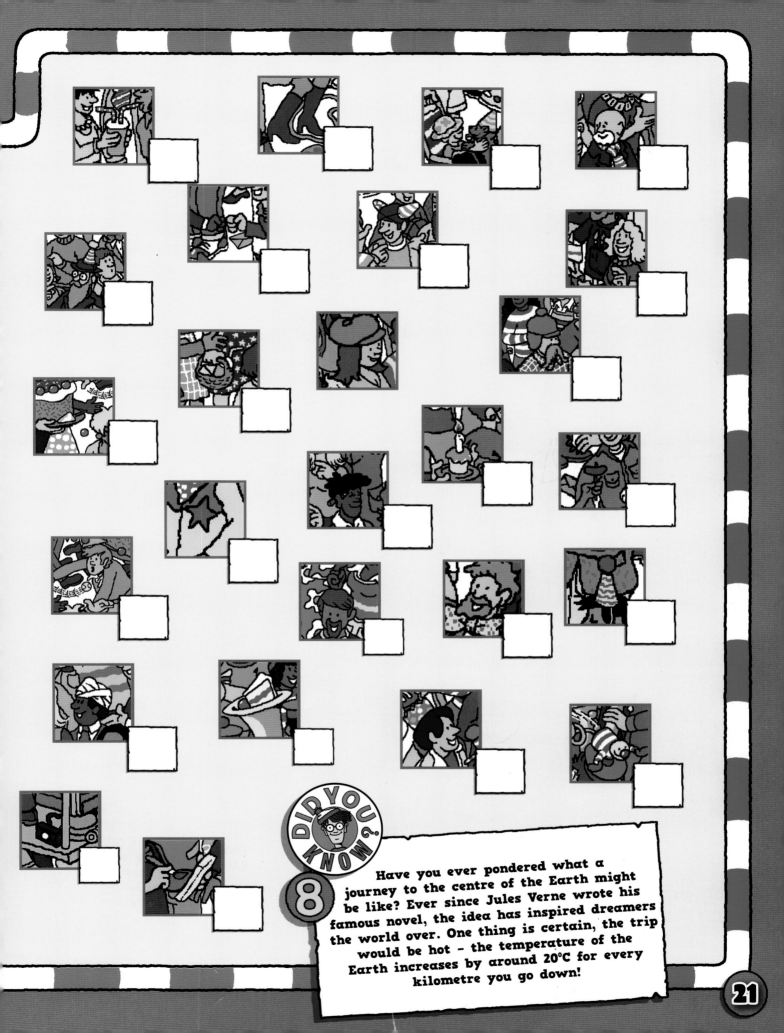

21

ON THE WRITE TRACK

Postcards aren't just for holidays, they're the perfect way of reaching family and friends all year round! When we see a postcard on our doormat, we can be instantly transported to a far-flung corner of the world. When it comes to penning postcards, Wally is a grandmaster; now you can be too with these top tips on creating your own . . .

You will need:
- Pencil
- Ruler
- White art card
- Old magazines
- Scissors
- Felt-tip pens
- Paper glue
- Glitter
- Sticky-back plastic

1. Cut a piece of white card to the size of a postcard (105 x 148 mm).
2. Decide where your postcard will be from. The picture doesn't have to show your own town, in fact, the only limit is your imagination. What would a postcard look like if it came from a deep sea submarine, a world full of dinosaurs, or outer space?
3. Cut out or draw pictures that fit your theme. Use paper glue to make a collage on one side, adding in doodles with felt-tip pens.

Why not draw pictures of everyone you have met on your travels?

Send Wally a postcard! Wally is an avid postcard reader – send him a picture of your postcard creation and it might even be featured on the Where's Wally? website! To find out the details log on to www.findwally.co.uk

4. When your design is ready, carefully laminate it with sticky-back plastic. Postcards don't have envelopes to protect them, so they need to be sturdy enough to make it safely through the post. Cover the picture side with the plastic.

5. Now, write your message and the recipient's address on the reverse. The trick to a good postcard is to fill it with local flavour. You only have a few short sentences to make the recipient feel what it's like to be with you. Start by setting the scene, include a funny story and pick out things you know they might be interested in. Use all your senses to explain the world around you: the smell of cooking food, the colours of fireworks blazing through the sky, or the feel of the sand running through your toes.

The official name for collecting postcards is deltiology. The curious term comes from the Greek word deltos, meaning writing tablet or letter.

Why not write your postcard with some pictures dotted among your very creative memories of your holiday?

Wally

To:
The Occupier
The House
The Street
The Town
The Land
The World

The first postcards were sent not long after 1840, when the first sticky postage stamp, the Penny Black, was issued. Since then, cards have been sent in their millions.

DID YOU KNOW?

9

Every Valentine's Day, William Shakespeare's tragic heroine Juliet is mailed about 1,000 love letters and cards. The messages are addressed to her in Verona, the northern Italian city where the play, Romeo and Juliet, is set.

A-MAZING

Wally has stumbled across an a-mazing maze of epic proportions! Woof has padded on ahead, but now he is lost somewhere amongst the labyrinth's dead-ends, tight turns and blind alleys. Even the well-meaning Wally Watchers on every corner can't point their hero in the right direction.

It's up to you to help Wally find his displaced dog! Trace your way through the maze's tangled paths, until you reach the centre. Once you've got to Woof, guide him safely to the exit.

START

DID YOU KNOW?

It is believed that the first ever recorded labyrinth wasn't the mythical home of the Minotaur in Ancient Crete, but a vast maze built in Egypt in the 5th century BCE. When he visited, the Greek travel-writer Herodotus claimed that the maze was even more impressive than the great pyramids.

FINISH

KEEP IT UNDER YOUR HAT

The distance between Wally and Odlaw is closing up fast! Now the race to reach Wally is on, but will it be you that finds him first? Wally's left you a clue to help you on your way, based on a code that he keeps under his bobble hat. Study the key code below, then match the letters of the alphabet to the secret hieroglyphics.

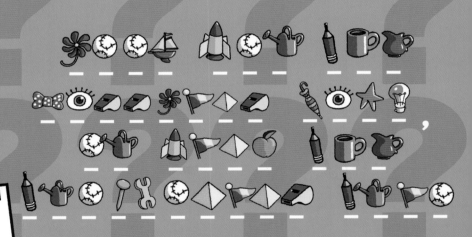

LOOK ~~FOR~~ ~~THE~~ _ _ _

_ _ _ _ _ _

_ _ _ , _ _ _

_ _ _ _ _

_ _ _ _

CRACKING CODES

It isn't just Wally who likes to send secret signals – codes and ciphers have been in use for thousands of years! Here in the digital age, codes are everywhere! ATM machines, broadband and supermarket tills all use encryption – the modern world couldn't function without it.

Morse code

Most people have heard of Morse code, but not many realise that it isn't actually a code at all – it's an electro-magnetic telegraph system. Morse translates the alphabet into sounds that can be sent over great distances, with a dash equalling the length of three dots. If you wanted to send a secret message in Morse code, you'd need to code it first!

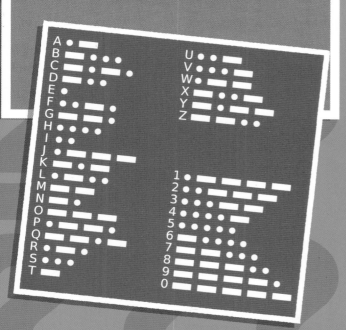

Don't shoot the messenger

In 405 BCE, the Greek General Lysander of Sparta was sent a secret message etched on the inside of a belt. When he wound the belt around a pole, the letters revealed that the Persians were about to attack. As a result, Lysander rallied his troops and defeated his enemies first.

DID YOU KNOW?

Weak ciphers cost lives! In the 16th century, Mary Queen of Scots paid the ultimate price when she penned coded letters, urging her supporters to assassinate Queen Elizabeth I. Disaster struck when the treacherous notes were intercepted by the head of the secret service, Sir Francis Walsingham, who cracked the code easily. Mary was executed for her crime.

SURPRISING TIMES

After an epic adventure that's been 25 years in the making, Wally deserves a celebration party that thrills on a global scale! Preparations are at fever pitch, but one big question looms large - can the eternal rambler stop rambling long enough to join in the fun?

"OK, people, let's focus!"

John, the party director, put down his megaphone and waited for the throng of bobble hats around him to hush. Countless Wally Watchers stood in the main street, milling in anxious circles as far as the eye could see.

"Thank you," said John, when the crowd finally fell silent. "First off, has anyone here seen Wally recently?"

An enormous, ear-splitting hubbub immediately broke out. The Wally Watchers scratched their heads and waved maps, shouting out a dozen different locations. Could Wally really have been spotted surfing with sharks and playing croquet with kangaroos?

Or did the Wally Watcher who was claiming he'd been kidnapped by Martians really have a point?

"I'll file that under work-in-progress for now," John decided, making a note on his clipboard. "Let's go back to the invitations. Have they all been sent?"

John tugged his beard a little nervously. The director had pulled off countless big film productions in his time, but organising this surprise party for Wally was proving to be a huge challenge.

John thought back to the last time he'd seen Wally, strolling casually across the set of his award-winning epic, *Zombies in Paris*! The director had immediately spotted the traveller's red and white hat bobbing through the set's torn tricolores and broken barricades. John was impressed by the effortless way Wally dodged disaster and always with a smile. From that day on they became firm friends - making the famous director the natural choice to stage-manage Wally's anniversary party.

"John!" interrupted a voice. "Yoo-hoo. Over here please!"

John and the Wally Watchers spun round. There, on the other side of the street, the chef Marcel was waving at them from the top of a very precarious stepladder.

"My creation is nearly ready!" he announced proudly. "I have created the prince of patisserie! Twenty-five layers of mouth-watering, *délicieux* celebration cake!"

The chef gestured to the enormous anniversary gateaux towering behind him, adding a final cherry with an artistic flourish.

"Very good!" smiled John, delighted to place at least one tick on his checklist. "No matter when he arrives, I'm sure Wally's going to love it."

The colour drained from Marcel's face.

"When he arrives?" he replied curtly. "*When* he arrives? I do all zis for nothing?!"

The director held up his hands. "It's just taking a little longer than planned to get an invite to our guest of honour ..."

Marcel flung his piping bag down in disgust. "This cake, my *oeuvre*, is filled with twenty-five layers of whipped cream. It 'as to be eaten within a few days or ..."

"Stay calm, Marcel!" gasped John. If he didn't get a break soon, Wally's surprise party was going to boast the biggest surprise yet – no Wally!

Suddenly, a young Wally Watcher elbowed his way to the front of crowd.

"Hey, sir, look!" he cried. "I've got a postcard!"

The director gave the lad a slap on the back.

"We've got a lead, folks!" he yelled. "I need a group of you to deliver an invitation to wherever in Cuba this card was postmarked."

Twenty-five loyal Wally Watchers sprinted out of the street.

"Don't forget to keep our cover!" John called after them. "Write and tell Wally he's needed here to renew his passport. We can't spoil the surprise."

Twenty-five hands gave an optimistic thumbs-up. Now all John had to do was sort out the streamers , music and balloons ...

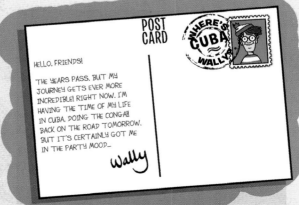

POST CARD

HELLO, FRIENDS!

THE YEARS PASS. BUT MY JOURNEY GETS EVER MORE INCREDIBLE! RIGHT NOW, I'M HAVING THE TIME OF MY LIFE IN CUBA, DOING THE CONGA!! BACK ON THE ROAD TOMORROW. BUT IT'S CERTAINLY GOT ME IN THE PARTY MOOD...

Wally

WHERE'S CUBA WALLY

While the director organised his party planners, the other Wally Watchers scoured South America. Aside from learning to ride with gauchos, tango in the twilight and make a mean chilli, they discovered something else – pinning down Wally is practically impossible!

A day or so later, a tanned Wally fan tapped John on the shoulder.

"I was on my way to the party," she beamed. "When I found this card from the great man himself!"

John took the postcard and started to read.

John slapped his forehead – Wally had been too quick for them again! Guests were streaming in and the street was getting busier by the hour.

"Let's just keep mailing those postcards," said the director with an optimistic smile. "The Wally Watchers network spreads far and wide. Someone's got to bump into him soon."

But, as afternoon galloped into early evening, a legion of Wally Watchers turned up, carrying armfuls of returned post. Every card they'd tried to send to Wally had boomeranged back – 'NOT AT THIS ADDRESS' stamped across the front in big letters.

John made a bolt for his trailer.

The director was lying on his sofa with a damp flannel over his eyes when his laptop started to flash.

"What now?" he groaned, reaching for it.

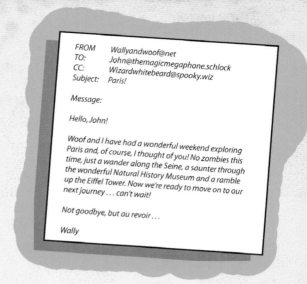

FROM   Wallyandwoof@net
TO: John@themagicmegaphone.schlock
CC: Wizardwhitebeard@spooky.wiz
Subject: Paris!

Message:

Hello, John!

Woof and I have had a wonderful weekend exploring Paris and, of course, I thought of you! No zombies this time, just a wander along the Seine, a saunter through the wonderful Natural History Museum and a ramble up the Eiffel Tower. Now we're ready to move on to our next journey . . . can't wait!

Not goodbye, but au revoir . . .

Wally

John slapped the laptop shut and tore out of the trailer.

"Wally's in Europe!" he bellowed. "He's getting closer!"

"Zat is a relief," replied Marcel, spritzing his cake with icing sugar. "The band 'ave just turned up."

And what a band it was. Tailing down the street, round the bend and into the distance was the longest line of

musicians John had ever seen. There was brass from Bolton, an oompah outfit from Bavaria, jazz singers from New Orleans and a circle of steel pans from Trinidad. The musicians started to parp, bang and toot.

"Tuning a band this size takes some puff," shouted the bandmaster. "They can't keep that kind of sound going forever, you know."

Suddenly one of the tubas began to splutter and screech. The crowd gasped as a small grey bird began to wriggle out from the inside of the instrument's bell!

"It's a homing pigeon," cried John.

Slowly and carefully, he opened the little tag fixed to the bird's leg.

GETTING IN TOUCH BY AIRMAIL WHILST RIDING THE FERRY! THE WHITE CLIFFS OF DOVER ARE LOOMING INTO SIGHT . . .
UNTIL NEXT TIME

Wally

"Strike up the band!" cheered John. "Wally's coming!"

The bandmaster tried to call his musicians to order, but Marcel wasn't impressed.

"If he's coming home," he shouted indignantly, "where is 'e?"

John peered up and down the street. Wally was still nowhere to be seen.

An hour later, things were looking bleak. John was trying to find the courage to call the whole thing off, when his assistant suddenly elbowed his way through the crowd.

"For you, sir!" he bellowed, thrusting a mobile phone into John's hand. "It's been beeping like crazy!"

The director sighed and took the phone, expecting to see a message from his wife, Deborah . . .

"It's a text," stuttered John. "From Wally!"

WALLYCOM

WALKING THROUGH A NEW PART OF TOWN WHERE THE STREETS ARE FILLED WITH MUSIC! MUST DASH – WOOF AND I HAVE GOT A VERY IMPORTANT DATE. TTFN,
WALLY

The packed street fell silent, craning to catch every word. Inexplicably, enchantingly, the atmosphere seemed to crackle with excitement. Could Wally really be just round the corner?

John raised the megaphone to his mouth one last time.

"Wally Watchers, guests and friends," he announced solemnly. "Let's get ready to party!"

Turn the page and see if you can find Wally at his celebration!

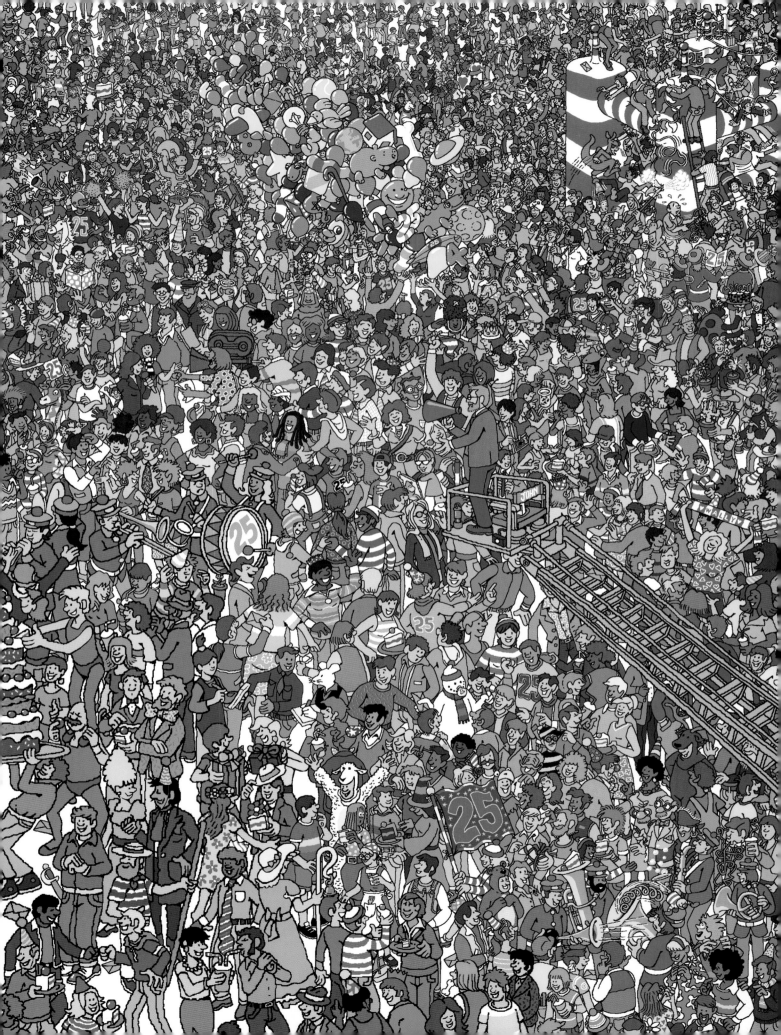

THE TRAVELLER'S TIMES

25p

SPOTTED?
STRIPY SIGHTINGS ARE STREAMING IN FROM AUSTRALIA TO ZANZIBAR!

Cover story by roving staff reporter **Wenda**.

Sources close to the *The Traveller's Times* have reported multiple sightings of rambling legend, Wally. Cables, telexes and tweets have been flooding in from all four corners of the globe, packed with sightings from such remote locations as Transylvania, Waikiki and Kathmandu.

As the days tick down to the 25th anniversary of the beginning of Wally's fantastic journey, a growing sense of anticipation is building up amongst Wally Watchers everywhere.

Excitement was first sparked when a trek guide in Tibet claimed to have spotted a stripy bobble-hatted individual hiking through a remote mountain pass of the Himalayas, with only a yak for company. Wally fans had to wait an anxious two weeks for the witness to make his way back down to the nearest base camp so he could be questioned in more detail. Yet when pressed, the guide backtracked, suggesting that he may have been suffering from mild altitude sickness at the time of the sighting.

The world's imagination was whetted however, and more reports started flooding in on a daily basis.

Here in the UK, Mr Sidney Harper, of 2 The Ridings, Tunbridge Wells, claimed that a gentleman looking very much like Wally had delivered his pint of milk that very morning. When your enquiring reporter went to the scene, Mr Harper's neighbours expressed some doubt about the authenticity of the claim. The self-confessed curtain-twitcher's dawn sighting coincided with a uniform change at the local dairy. Possibly the most conclusive moment came when a local souvenir seller took this snap of a man alone outside the Taj Mahal Palace in India. The seller sold the photo to a journalist for a hefty sum, before uploading the shot onto the Internet for the world to scrutinise.

Could this distant pose finally be a creditable sighting of Wally? The photo is impressive, but the blurry image and shadowy light seems to raise more questions than it does answers.

Are the Wally Watchers finally getting close to tracking down their elusive hero? Nobody knows the traveller's precise location or whether he will even make it to the impressive anniversary celebrations scheduled for just a few days' time! Like a will-o'-the-wisp, the legend seems to walk amongst us, slipping away before our very eyes!

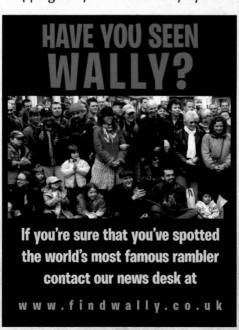

HAVE YOU SEEN WALLY?

If you're sure that you've spotted the world's most famous rambler contact our news desk at

w w w . f i n d w a l l y . c o . u k

SPORTS NEWSFLASH!

The Ashes cricket test match in Sydney, Australia was interrupted yesterday by a curious pitch invasion. Just before tea, a little white dog was seen to trot through the slips across silly mid-off, and out past the third man before disappearing into the pavilion at the Syndey Cricket Ground.

Before the umpire could stop play, the pet had disappeared. Several fans took photos, but a glimpse of a stripy tail was the best snap that could be mustered. Aussie bowler Shane Bundy later blamed the mysterious mutt for an embarrassing series of no-balls. Turn to the back page for a full match report.

PUZZLE
OF THE DAY
Picture Sudoku

It's a Wally news day, so our puzzle is crammed with travelling kit! Can you fill in the Sudoku squares? Draw the correct pieces of kit into the grid, making sure that no picture is repeated in the same column, row or block.

ODLAW AT LARGE

The Traveller's Times can reveal that the notorious rascal Odlaw continues to elude police, in a troubling turn of bungles, botches and false arrests. The criminal is still on the run, out-smarting the good guys time and time again.

A photo-fit of Odlaw has been circulated by Interpol, but the infamous crook needs little introduction. His bumblebee-striped top and handlebar moustache would stand out in any crowd.

For now there is just one question on everybody's lips: Where will the scoundrel show up next?

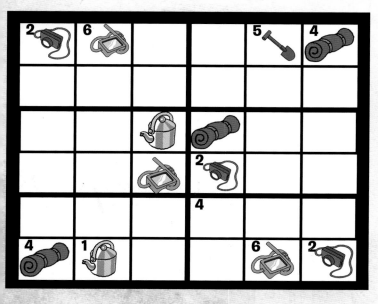

DID YOU KNOW?

12

The Traveller's Times is a must-read news-sheet, but the *Times of India* is even more widely consumed. Its circulation of around 3,146,000 issues a day makes it the most widely circulated daily in the English language. That's a lot of fish-and-chip papers!

A HAND FOR THE BAND

A legion of musicians turned out to make sure that Wally's street party went with a swing! Bandmasters, fiddlers, bagpipe-players and big-bass-drummers all tooted, banged and bashed in time to the tunes. No one had ever seen such a gathering of musical mavericks!

A complete British brass band is made up of at least 28 players, plus percussionists. The instruments range from cornets, flugelhorns and trombones, right through to tubas and euphoniums! There are no trumpets or French horns, however – these instruments are only included in traditional concert bands or orchestras.

Take a close look at these pictures of some of the performers. Can you spot 25 differences between them? Draw a circle around every one that you find.

What happened next?
The musicians marched on and the band kept playing . . . or did they? Grab a pencil and paper, then draw your own artist's impression of what happened when the entertainers conga-ed round the corner.

V.I.P. WORD SEARCH

People travelled far and wide to attend Wally's fantastic party! This letter grid holds the identities of 25 extra-special guests, a costumed clutch of V.I.P.s that stand out from the crowd. Can you find each and every one? First, study the picture clues. If you can't guess who's who, unscramble the anagrams and write the letters into the blank spaces below. Now it's time to hit the grid! The names could be running in any direction – horizontally, vertically, diagonally or back-to-front.

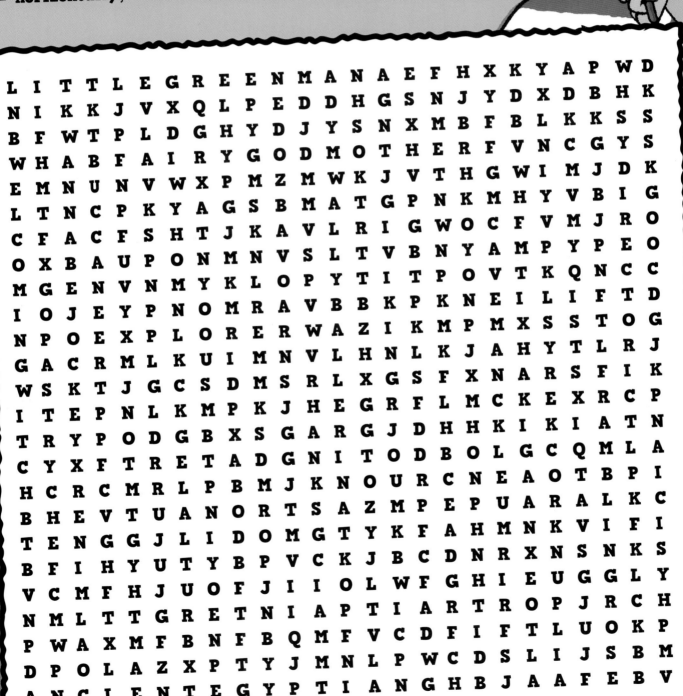

```
L I T T L E G R E E N M A N A E F H X K Y A P W D
N I K K J V X Q L P E D D H G S N J Y D X D B H K
B F W T P L D G H Y D J Y S N X M B F B L K K S S
W H A B F A I R Y G O D M O T H E R F V N C G Y S
E M N U V W X P M Z M W K J V T H G W I M J D K
L T N C P K Y A G S B M A T G P N K M H Y V B I G
C F A C F S H T J K A V L R I G W O C F V M J R O
O X B A U P O N M N V S L T V B N Y A M P Y P E O
M G E N V N M Y K L O P Y T I T P O V T K Q N C C
I O J E Y P N O M R A V B B K P K N E I L I F T D
N P O E X P L O R E R W A Z I K M P M X S S T O G
G A C R M L K U I M N V L H N L K J A H Y T L R J
W S K T J G C S D M S R L X G S F X N A R S F I K
I T E P N L K M P K J H E G R F L M C K E X R C P
T R Y P O D G B X S G A R G J D H H K I K I A T N
C Y X F T R E T A D G N I T O D B O L G C Q M L A
H C R C M R L P B M J K N O U R C N E A O T B P I
B H E V T U A N O R T S A Z M P E P U A R A L K C
T E N G G J L I D O M G T Y K F A H M N K V I F I
B F I H Y U T Y B P V C K J B C D N R X S N K S
V C M F H J U O F J I I O L W F G H I E U G G L Y
N M L T T G R E T N I A P T I A R T R O P J R C H
P W A X M F B N F B Q M F V C D F I F T L U O K P
D P O L A Z X P T Y J M N L P W C D S L I J S B M
A N C I E N T E G Y P T I A N G H B J A A F E B V
```

42

1. PURES REOH

----------- ---------

2. UNKP ROKERC

----- ------ ------

3. TNACNEI GAPIYENT

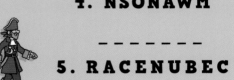

------- -------- -------

4. NSONAWM

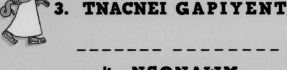

------- -------

5. RACENUBEC

--------- ----

6. GINODT RADET

------ ----- -----

7. ITLELT REGNE NMA

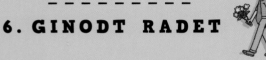

------ ------ ---

8. REKSAT OYB

------ ---

9. LAYWL NALIBELAR

----- ---------

10. NISHPAYIC

----

11. TANSURTOA

----

12. MEGWIOLNC TIHWC

--------- ---------

13. PHIYP KICCH

----- ------ ---

14. NIVKGI

------ ------

15. MBIRGANL SERO

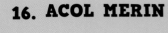

-------- --------- ----

16. ACOL MERIN

----- ------

17. RETCODRI

----

18. OCW LIGR

--- ----

19. RITRATPO APITREN

-------- ---------

20. XRELOPER

----

21. YAFRI MOHDERGOT

----- ------- -------

22. VACENAM

------- -----

23. PSYART FECH

------ ----

24. BORTO

-----

25. ENAWANB YECKOJ

------- ------

WIZARD WHITEBEARD'S MAGIC SCROLL

Wizard Whitebeard has cast a spell to charm Wally on his latest journey, scribing it onto a special anniversary scroll. As is always the way with the wily wizard, there's more to this incantation than first meets the eye! Set deep within the magical verse are 25 mystery locations from all around this great globe.

Spell-searchers will need to pore over every syllable. All places uttered in the Wizard's spell sound correct, but not every one is spelt as it would be if tracked down in an atlas. The scroll hides puns, double meanings and words within words. The first three are marked to help you – happy hunting for the rest!

There is yet one more message hidden in the soothsayer's spell. Look up, look down, then write the message here.

– –

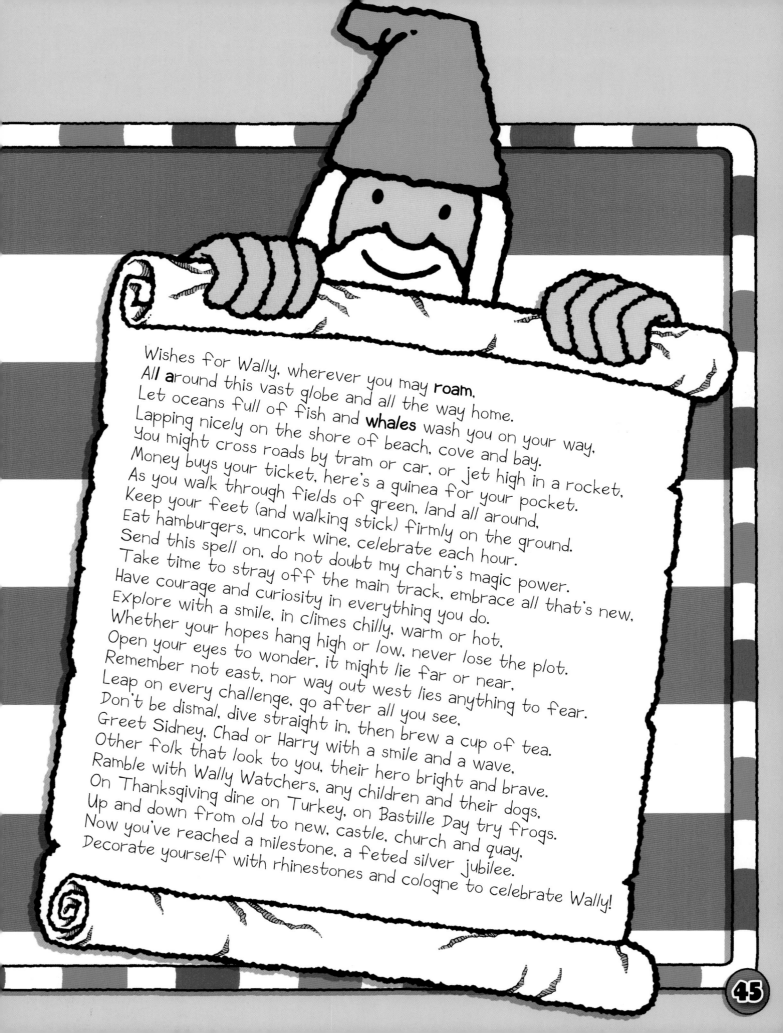

Wishes for Wally, wherever you may **roam**,
All around this vast globe and all the way home.
Let oceans full of fish and **whales** wash you on your way,
Lapping nicely on the shore of beach, cove and bay.
You might cross roads by tram or car, or jet high in a rocket,
Money buys your ticket, here's a guinea for your pocket.
As you walk through fields of green, land all around,
Keep your feet (and walking stick) firmly on the ground.
Eat hamburgers, uncork wine, celebrate each hour.
Send this spell on, do not doubt my chant's magic power.
Take time to stray off the main track, embrace all that's new,
Have courage and curiosity in everything you do.
Explore with a smile, in climes chilly, warm or hot,
Whether your hopes hang high or low, never lose the plot.
Open your eyes to wonder, it might lie far or near,
Remember not east, nor way out west lies anything to fear.
Leap on every challenge, go after all you see,
Don't be dismal, dive straight in, then brew a cup of tea.
Greet Sidney, Chad or Harry with a smile and a wave,
Other folk that look to you, their hero bright and brave.
Ramble with Wally Watchers, any children and their dogs,
On Thanksgiving dine on Turkey, on Bastille Day try frogs.
Up and down from old to new, castle, church and quay,
Now you've reached a milestone, a feted silver jubilee.
Decorate yourself with rhinestones and cologne to celebrate Wally!

MARVELLOUS MAPS

Maps are more than mere charts showing the lay of the land. Each one tells us about the map-maker and the times he or she lived in. Wally is happy to wander wherever his walking stick takes him, but the world wouldn't spin so efficiently if we didn't have maps to guide us through our lives.

A brief history of maps . . .
We've been trying to chart the world around us for millennia - cartography in ancient times was much more advanced than you might expect! The ancient Greek philosophers were convinced that the world was spherical, hundreds of years before the explorers of the 15th century.

T and O maps
During Medieval times, the accuracy of maps went backwards! Cartographers placed Jerusalem and the Holy Lands in the centre of their maps, arranging the other land masses in the middle of a T-shaped area of ocean. Not many people got to see these works - each map had to be individually drawn, making them extremely rare and valuable items.

Sail the seven seas
In Renaissance times, merchants and traders became more adventurous, heralding another leap of progress for mapping. Ships charted coastlines, using the stars and compasses to navigate their routes across the seas. Printing also developed, making maps much more plentiful.

Peters Projection

Representing a round planet on a flat piece of paper was never going to be easy, but the Peters Projection world map in 1974 caused controversy.

It is impossible to show both the size and shape of the land masses at the same time. The Peters Projection shows all areas according to their accurate size.

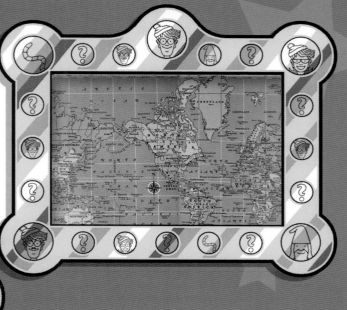

Mapping the Moon

Scientists are working hard to create highly detailed maps of the Moon. When the charts are produced, they will be on a larger scale than the Ordnance Survey maps that ramblers use here on Earth!

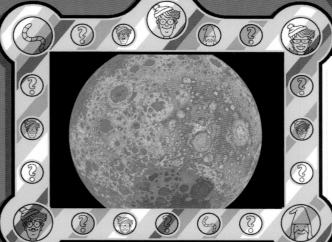

Modern maps

Nowadays maps are unrecognisable from those of our forebears. Cartographers now rely on a huge range of data including remote sensing and GIS (Geographic Information Systems) computer software, taking mapping to a whole new level.

DID YOU KNOW? 17

The oldest surviving maps were discovered in Mesopotamia, etched onto clay tablets that had been dried in the sun. Other ancient peoples carved their maps on mosaic tiles. Later parchment maps devised by the Greeks and Romans were more lightweight and portable, but they didn't stand the test of time. The fragile papers have perished over the centuries.

WALLY'S GREAT GLOBAL CHALLENGE

How well do you know this big wide world of ours? Grab a pencil and pit your wits in this challenge. This global quiz is packed with brilliant brainteasers and even the most worldly-wise Wally Watcher might need an atlas to help them!

1 The Vatican City is the world's smallest country. Which Italian city is it in?

....

2 North versus South! Which is the biggest hemisphere?

....

3 Which of these countries doesn't have French as its official language?

A. Cameroon
B. Mauritius
C. Senegal

4 Which is the largest city on the planet?

A. Paris
B. New York
C. Shanghai

5 Where was the venue of the last Winter Olympic Games?

A. Vancouver
B. Edinburgh
C. Montreal

6 What is the capital city of Switzerland?

A. Geneva
B. Bern
C. Basel

7 The world's deepest lake is Lake Baikal, but which country is it in?

A. Canada
B. Russia
C. China

8 We all know about Everest, but Mauna Kea is a contender for the world's tallest mountain if measured from its ocean base. Which island is it on?

A. Hawaii
B. Cyprus
C. Guernsey

9 Which continent does the Nile river flow through?

....

10 Place a tick next to the world's driest inhabited place.

A. Sahara Desert, Africa
B. Ica, Peru
C. Aswan, Egypt

11 How far is Cornwall's Land's End from New York City?

....

12 Which is the world's most populated continent?

....

13 Which four countries make up the United Kingdom?

....

14 Which three colours form the German flag?

....

15 Australia boasts such colourfully named towns as Humpy Doo, Wagga Wagga and Geelong.

True or false?

16 Which country has been celebrating the Day of the Dead Festival for over 3,500 years?

A. Mexico
B. Peru
C. Chile

17 What is the capital of Malaysia?

A. Ipoh
B. Kuching
C. Kuala Lumpur

18 The world's youngest island is called Surtsey, created in 1963 by an undersea volcano. Where is it?

....

19 Unscramble these anagrams of countries:

TANGO _ _ _ _ _

20 PLANE _ _ _ _ _

21 MOAN _ _ _ _

22 Where is Santa said to live?

....

23 With over 40 floods a year and counting, Venice is sinking fast! What is the city also known as?

A. City of Bridges
B. City of Rains
C. City of Canals

24 How many countries in the world are there today?

....

25 The Great Wall of China is truly vast, but can it really be spotted from space?

....

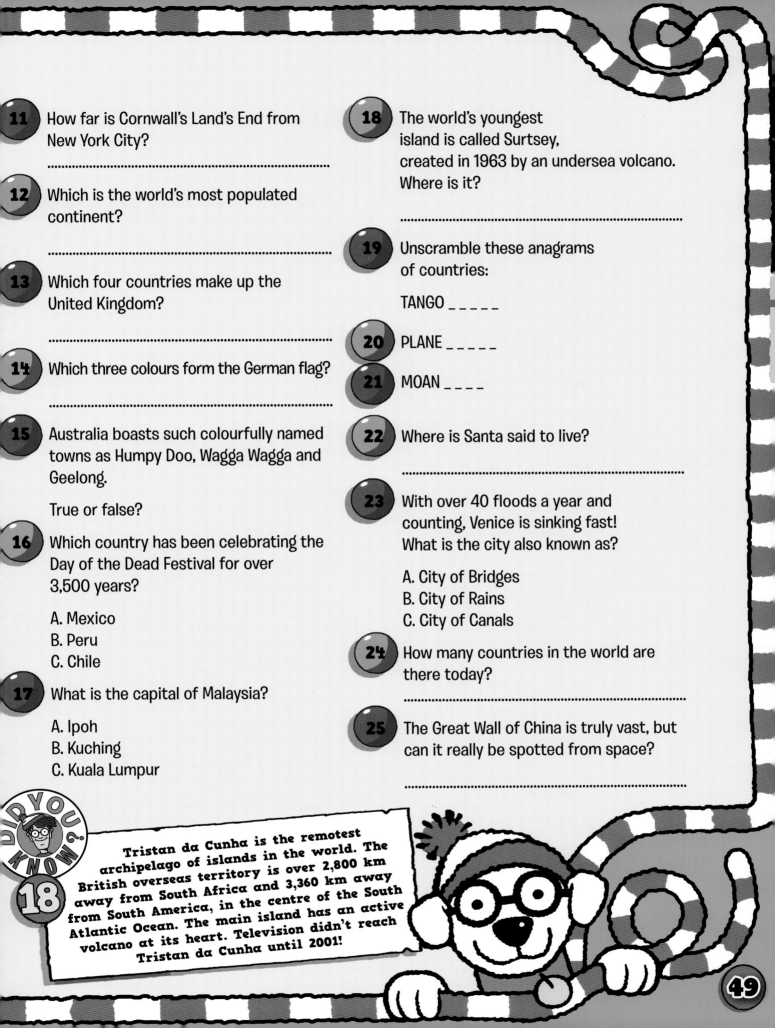

DID YOU KNOW?

18 Tristan da Cunha is the remotest archipelago of islands in the world. The British overseas territory is over 2,800 km away from South Africa and 3,360 km away from South America, in the centre of the South Atlantic Ocean. The main island has an active volcano at its heart. Television didn't reach Tristan da Cunha until 2001!

MAKE YOUR OWN
TRAVEL JOURNAL

A journal is essential kit for any world traveller – it's a diary, photo album, sketchpad and scrapbook all-in-one! Next time you go on an exciting journey, pop a notebook in your rucksack, or make a journal to take with you. Soon you'll have a row of unique travelogues lining your bookshelf!

1. Start by decorating your cardboard. This will be your cover, so make it eye-catching. Paint pictures that encapsulate the feel of the place you're visiting. Embellish your designs with glitter, gel pens, pressed flowers or collage pieces, then laminate both pieces with sticky-back plastic. Why not add a picture of home on the back cover?

2. Stick a strong envelope on the reverse side of your front cover to make a handy storage pouch for the souvenirs you collect on your travels!

You will need:
- Two A5 sheets of cardboard (148 x 210 mm)
- Paint, pens, collage items and glitter
- Scissors
- PVA glue
- Sticky-back plastic
- At least 20 separate sheets of paper cut to A5 size
- Hole punch
- Wooden chopstick
- Sandpaper
- Plain elastic hair band

3. The sheets of paper will form the inside pages of your travel journal. Why not use a variety of different colours and weights?

4. Use a hole punch to make two holes in the shorter edge of the paper pages and card covers, to make a landscape book.

5. Carefully cut a chopstick in half, then use sandpaper to smooth down the broken end.

Travel-writing tips

Little and often
Don't recount every detail of your day, just the things that capture your imagination. An interesting encounter or an unforgettable sight will instantly transport the reader to the place that you're describing.

Look out for souvenirs
Stick or store souvenirs you collect as you go. Tickets, maps and postcards will bring your trip to life when you get back home.

Write what you see
Jot down the sights, sounds and smells of your new location. Observe the locals and make note of anything that fascinates you. These golden nuggets will make wonderful reading later.

Messages from far-flung friends
If you meet new friends on your trip, ask them to write a message for you, or their own thoughts about the location you're enjoying. Don't forget to ask them for their contact details so you can keep in touch!

6. Put your front and back covers around your pages, lining them all up. Turn the journal over, stretch a hair band along the back of the book and push the ends of it through the holes in the back cover and out through the front.

7. Slip the chopstick through the two loops of hair band that have come through to the front of the cover. The chopstick will be held in place vertically, binding your journal together!

8. Your journal is ready to use. If you fill it up, you can simply remove the chopstick binder and insert extra pages inside.

QUIZZICAL QUEUES

Wally's party-going pals are queuing up to shake the great man's hand and pat his lovable pooch, Woof. The over-excited revellers have tried to form orderly queues, but it's not always clear who's next in line. Who comes next in each of these patterns?

STRIPES RULE, OK!

Wally's distinctive look has been copied countless times. No one, it seems, can get enough of stripes! Whether you like to hang a candy cane on your Christmas tree, wear a Breton jumper or pull on stripy socks, you're invited to join in Wally's super-duper stripy celebration!

STRIPY SIGHTS

The Capanile of the Duomo in Siena, Italy
The striped Capanile or belltower of Siena's cathedral is built from alternated layers of greenish black-and-white marble. Black and white are the symbolic colours of the city.

Costa Nova, Portugal
Wally would feel at home amongst the eye-catching houses that lie along this section of Portuguese coast! The buildings were once fisherman's shacks, painted in bright colours so that they stood out against the sand.

Las Ramblas, Barcelona, Spain
Barcelona's famous walkway runs for 1.2 km from Plaça Catalunya in the centre to the Christopher Columbus monument at Port Vell. Many sections of the route are paved in head-turning black-and-white stripes.

Naturally stripy
Zebras and tigers are just two animal species that have evolved eye-catching stripy markings. Although the stripes look distinctive to humans, they actually work as an excellent form of camouflage. It is even thought that a group of zebras will use their markings to trick would-be attackers, blending together as if they are one single animal rather than a herd.

Flag-tastic!

Stripes are a hit the world over! Fill in the missing letters to name the countries that feature stripes in their flags.

_ E T _ _ R L _ ND _

_ U S S _ _

H _ _ G A _ _

_ _ _ TA R _ _ A

A _ _ EN _ I N _

_ U ST _ _ _

_ _ _ NC _

I _ EL _ _ D

_ _ MAN _ A

Stripes in art

Artists through the ages have used stripes to make an impact! In the 1940s and 1950s a school of painting emerged in New York called Color Field art. Many of the most famous Colour Field painters made major bodies of work based on stripes.

The greats have experimented with stripes too. Renoir's *La Loge* oil painting shows a lady at the opera dressed in a striking black-and-white gown, whilst Picasso's bold use of colour and stripes turned the world of art on its head. Other artists such as Bridget Riley and Giovanni Costa have also incorporated stripes into their paintings.

Renoir

Giovanni Costa

Picasso

Stripes to spot in everyday life

ISBN 978-1-40930-920-8
9 781409 309208
Barcodes

Zebra crossings

Ranks in the armed forces

DID YOU KNOW?

21

The most stripy fast food company has to be the US chain Whataburger. The restaurants all feature pitched orange-and-white striped roofs! The first Whataburger was opened in Corpus Christi, Texas by Harman Dobson. The magnate's goal was to serve a burger so big that it took two hands to hold, tasting so good that with one bite customers would say, "What a burger!"

WALLY'S WILD GOOSE CHASE

Don't expect to sit down for long on this page, Wally's wacky game will have you gallivanting all over the house! You and your friends are in a race to make it from the start of the party parade through to the end, but there are 25 challenges to deal with first. Can you find the items and bring them back to the game table without forfeiting your turn?

How to play

Ask your friends to choose a counter each, then place them on the start panel. The person who throws the highest number with the die gets to go first. Take turns to make your way along the squares, stopping every time you land on a red CHALLENGE square. You now have sixty seconds to find the item listed, bringing your trophy back to the table. If you can't fulfill the challenge, miss two turns. The player that gets to the finish first is the winner!

You will need:
- A die
- A stopwatch
- 1-3 pals to play with

DID YOU KNOW? 22

Many board games have battled it out for the top spot, but Hasbro's Monopoly has be one of the most enduring and widely played in the world. The property game is available in 111 countries and 43 languages! The highest value properties vary according to where the players live – in Spain a Barcelona street called Paseo del Prado is the most pricey. In France it's Rue de la Paix.

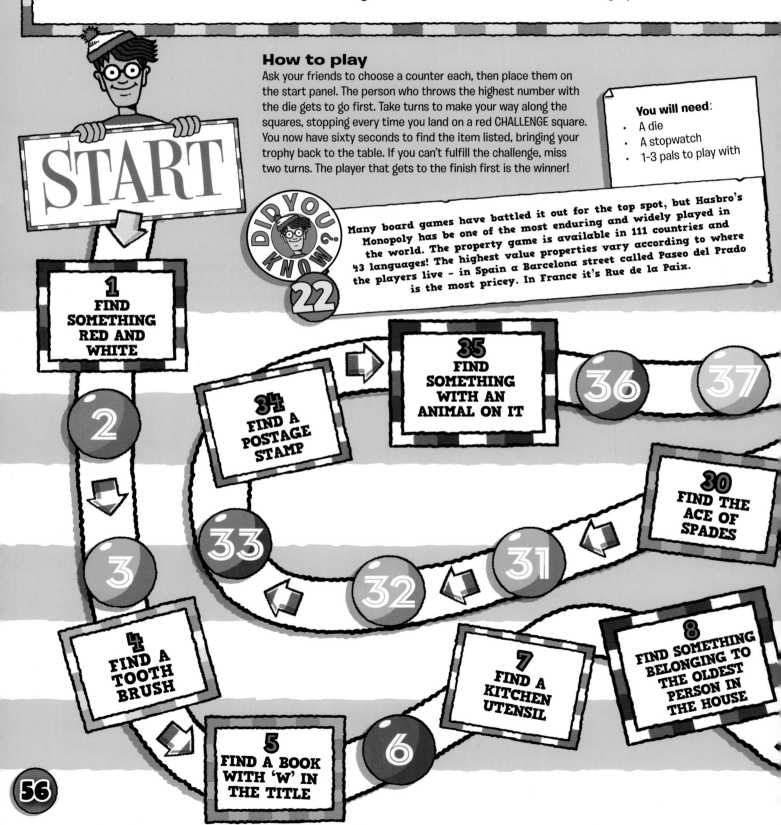

START

1 FIND SOMETHING RED AND WHITE

2

3

4 FIND A TOOTH BRUSH

5 FIND A BOOK WITH 'W' IN THE TITLE

6

7 FIND A KITCHEN UTENSIL

8 FIND SOMETHING BELONGING TO THE OLDEST PERSON IN THE HOUSE

30 FIND THE ACE OF SPADES

31

32

33

34 FIND A POSTAGE STAMP

35 FIND SOMETHING WITH AN ANIMAL ON IT

36

37

FINISH

48

49
FIND SOMETHING OVER 20 YEARS OLD

50
FIND AN OBJECT THAT'S SMALLER THAN YOUR THUMBNAIL

47
FIND A SWEET TREAT

46

45

44
FIND SOMETHING FROM A FOREIGN COUNTRY

43
FIND A BELT BUCKLE

42

41
FIND A PICTURE OF SOMEONE FAMOUS

40

39
FIND SOMETHING SMELLY

38
FIND A RECEIPT

28
FIND A GIRL'S TOY

27

26

25
FIND A DEVILLISH DISGUISE

29

24
FIND A TEA BAG

22

23

21
FIND A REMOTE CONTROL

20

17

18

16
FIND A TRAVEL SOUVENIR

15
FIND A SNACK TO SHARE WITH ALL THE OTHER PLAYERS

19
FIND A HOLIDAY POSTCARD

14

11
FIND SOMETHING RED AND WHITE

12

13
FIND 2 ODD SOCKS

9

10

57

PICTURE THIS!

Are you crazy for crosswords? Potty about puzzles? This grid is packed with 25 party-themed words, but the clues have been artfully done. Instead of cryptic phrases, there is a small picture for every word that you need to fill in.

Handy hint:
If the star behind the picture clue is orange, then the answer is two words!

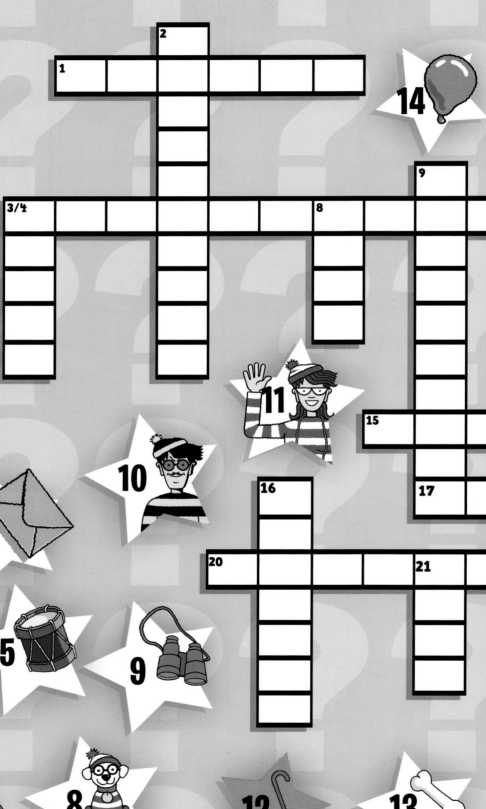

6

8

12

13

5

7

3

4

1

2

10

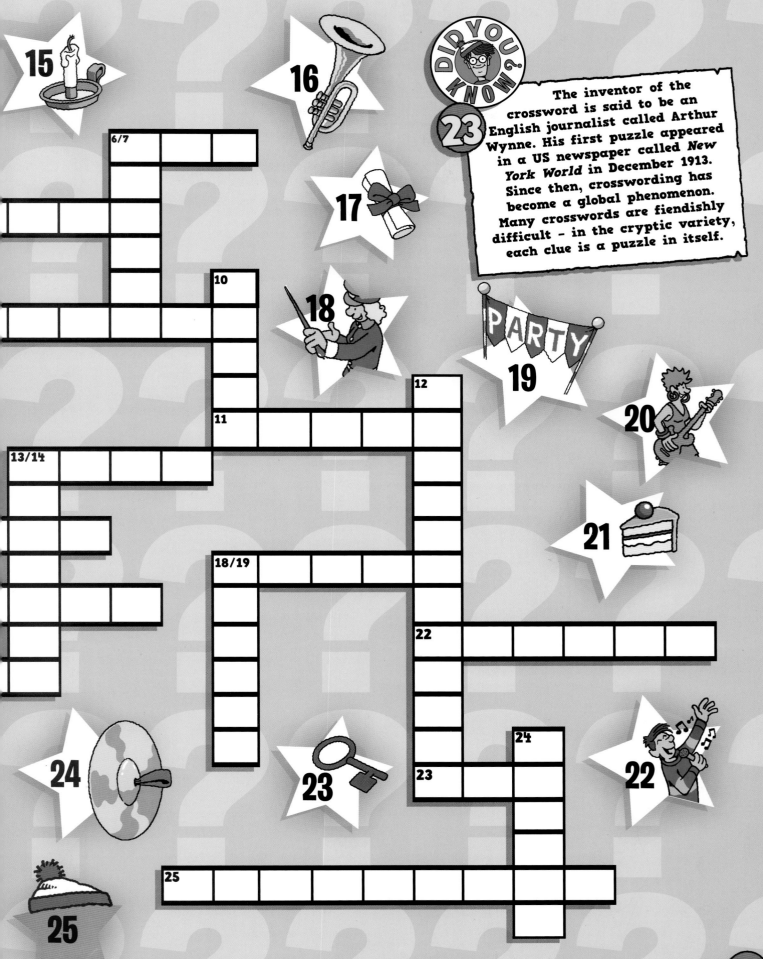

ANSWERS

P. 10 Puzzled Packing
1. SPONGE
2. MAGNIFYING GLASS
3. TORCH
4. PENCIL
5. RICE
6. POSTCARDS
7. TAPE
8. HARMONICA
9. PENNY
10. EAR PLUGS

P. 12 Down Memory Lane
1. WOOF
2. 5
3. PURPLE
4. LEFT
5. 5
6. PINK
7. YES
8. LOCKED
9. 9
10. SWEET
11. CLOSED
12. PINK
13. NORTH
14. STETHOSCOPE
15. GREEN
16. YELLOW
17. 6
18. 3, 5
19. RED
20. 7
21. Z, T, H
22. 3
23. ORANGE AND GREEN
24. 5
25. WALLY

P. 16 Balloon Game!
Wizard Whitebeard's balloon is tied to the red number 1 balloon.

P. 24 A-mazing Woof

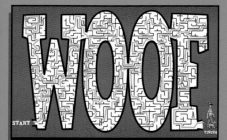

P. 26 Keep It Under Your Hat

LOOK FOR THE JUGGLING CUPS, OR FIND THE TROMBONING TRIO

P. 34-35 Traveller's Times

P. 40-41 A Hand for the Band

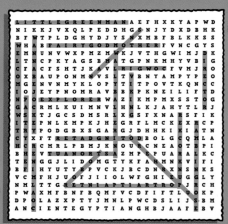

P. 42-43 V.I.P. Word Search

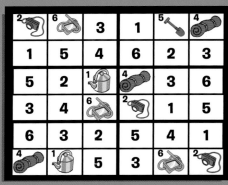

1. SUPER HERO
2. PUNK ROCKER
3. ANCIENT EGYPTIAN
4. SNOWMAN
5. BUCCANEER
6. DOTING DATER
7. LITTLE GREEN MAN
8. SKATER BOY
9. WALLY BALLERINA
10. PHYSICIAN
11. ASTRONAUT
12. WELCOMING WITCH
13. HIPPY CHICK
14. VIKING
15. RAMBLING ROSE
16. COAL MINER
17. DIRECTOR
18. COW GIRL
19. PORTRAIT PAINTER
20. EXPLORER
21. FAIRY GODMOTHER
22. CAVEMAN
23. PASTRY CHEF
24. ROBOT
25. WANNABE JOCKEY

P. 44-45 Wizard Whitebeard's Magic Scroll
WALLY MAKES THE WORLD GO ROUND

Wishes for Wally, wherever you may **roam**,
All around this vast globe and all the way home.
Let oceans full of **fish** and **whales** wash you on your way.
Lapping **nicely** on the shore of beach, cove and bay.
You might cross **roads** by tram or car, or **jet** high in a rocket.
Money buys you **tickets**, here's a **guinea** for your pocket.
As you walk through fields of **green**, **land** all around.
Keep your feet (and walking stick) firmly on the ground.
Eat **hamburgers**, **uncork** wine, celebrate each hour.
Send this spell **on**, do **not doubt** my chant's magic power.
Take time to stray off the **main** track, embrace all that's new.
Have courage and curiosity in everything you do.
Explore with a smile, in climes **chilly**, warm or hot,
Whether your hopes **hang high** or low, never lose the plot.
Open your eyes to wonder, it might lie **far** or near.
Remember not east, **nor way** out west lies anything to fear.
Leap on every challenge, **go after** all you see.
Don't be dismal, **dive straight** in, then brew a cup of tea.
Greet **Sidney**, **Chad** or Harry with a smile and a wave.
Other folk that look to you, their hero **brig** hb and brave.
Ramble with Wally Watchers, **any** children and their dogs.
On Thanksgiving dine on **Turkey**, on Bastille Day try frogs.
Up and down from old to **new**, **castle**, church and quay.
Now you've reached a milestone, a feted silver jubilee.
Decorate yourself with **rhinestones** and **cologne** to celebrate Wally!

P. 46-47 Wally's Great Global Challenge
1. Rome
2. At 99.9 million square kilometres, the Southern Hemisphere is bigger. The Northern Hemisphere is 48.9 million square kilometres
3. B: Mauritius
4. C: Shanghai
5. A: Vancouver
6. B: Bern
7. B: Russia
8. A: Hawaii
9. Africa
10. C: Aswan, Egypt
11. 5,064 km/3,147 m
12. Asia
13. England, Northern Island, Scotland and Wales
14. Black, red and gold
15. True
16. A: Mexico
17. C: Kuala Lumpur
18. Surtsey is off the south coast of Iceland.
19. Tonga
20. Nepal
21. Oman
22. North Pole
23. A: City of Bridges
24. There are approximately 195 countries, but only 192 are recognised by the United Nations
25. No, it's a myth

P. 52 Quizzical Queues
Snowman
Doting Dater
Little Green Man
Astronaut
Caveman

P. 55
Flag-tastic!
Netherlands
Russia
Hungary
Costa Rica
Argentina
Austria
France
Ireland
Romania

P. 58 Picture This!

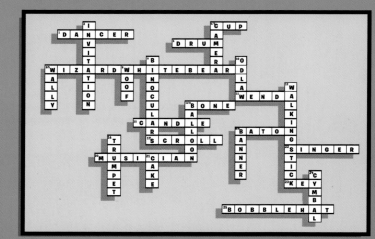

A FEW MORE THINGS...

Just when you thought you'd discovered all of this Annual's treasures, Wally has rustled up a final scavenger hunt! 25 more objects are buried in the pages of this book. It's up to you to unearth them all, placing a tick next to each one you track down.

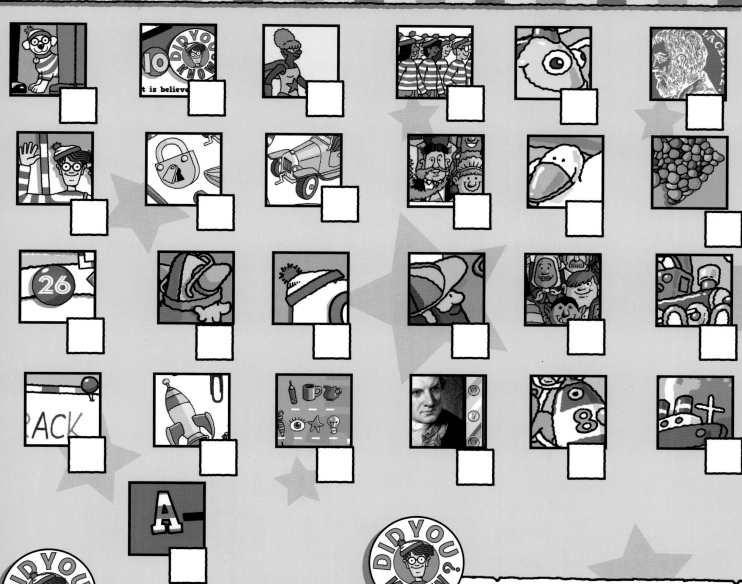